A Message to
Humanity

Eddy Colin

ISBN 979-8-89485-272-0 (Paperback)
ISBN 979-8-89485-273-7 (Digital)

Covenant Books
11661 Hwy 707
Murrells Inlet, SC 29576
www.covenantbooks.com

A Message to Humanity!

This message may be easily taken for granted by many, and to all those who may still have a flicker of light left within them, I call upon you as the children of light to understand the urgency of the time at hand on this last and final walk here on this earth. There are many who will not even come close to understanding the importance or magnitude of this very important final message from the divine God to His lost children. There are things in heaven and earth that neither you nor I will ever understand and must be left to God alone.

To all who can hear, be attentive and pay very close attention to the message that is being brought to your attention on these last days here and your last walk toward righteousness.

To all who can see, focus on the events that have taken place in these most recent times all over the world and reach deep within yourselves, and all the understanding and knowledge that have been planted deep within you all will intensify and awaken so your enlightenment may begin.

Don't ever lose focus on the purpose at hand for this last journey of the end of your life here. Today is of a magnitude on the greatest scale ever, and if you are not successful, you will lose your last chance of winning this great battle against the adversary—the devil. Most of us have lived the greatest portion of our lives here on earth, and many are still procrastinating—thinking daily about themselves as if they still have tomorrow and not realizing that the next minute may never come and miss the opportunity for salvation and redemption. My dear brothers and sisters, there is no guarantee of tomorrow; you must make your decision right now! I urge you! This is your last chance of redemption and a warning from the Most High through these words of truth in an attempt to reach you once again in a time that I believe to be most critical. How do I know this? I just know! Never shall I waver in my faith and doubt the guidance from the Holy Spirit within, who shall continue to give spiritual insight to me as I pass this message on to humanity. My friends, this is no coincidence that after the emergence of my first book, *My Struggles, My Bondage, and My Freedom and Deliverance*, which is about my own great battle, when God felt that I had enough, He pulled me out and set me on a new path, which I still am in.

This God of ours is so full of grace that, throughout time and history, He continues to reach out for us. Even as we continue to deny Him, He never stops loving us, and that, my friends, is unconditional love to the fullest. Until I started doing my own testimony as I gave out my books and business cards to people as guided by the Holy Spirit, I never had a clue on how many are truly in need of salvation and a better understanding of the love of God for them. It breaks my heart to know that so many of my friends have died without making the ultimate transformation in knowing God as I have gotten to know Him myself, and though they were friends of mine, there is nothing I could have done for them, for those who did not surrender to Jesus Christ before they died. Now my mission until I leave this earth for the rest of my days is to testify on behalf of my God as I give Him all the glory—well-deserved glory. I pray on this day as I embark on this worthy journey for strength and courage to carry on, that no obstacle shall stand in my way, and that mountains be moved before me, for I am extremely confident in the worthiness of humanity. If it were not so, God would have given up on us long ago. I pray that God helps me, gives me strength, keeps me only as safe as I need to be kept, and helps me see clearly enough to give all the glory to Him as my Father and as my Creator.

Movements in Heaven

I feel a motion of significance happening in heaven right now, as if something of major significance is taking place. I feel compelled to document this as a memo in my computer database. I am not yet sure why it needs to be so, but I am forced to document this anyway. Lately, I have been able to feel, and I can tell that the devil is very agitated. I can almost somewhat feel this other realm in ways that I am not yet able to explain fully, or maybe it is not for me to understand! But I can tell for sure that the time has come, and God is about to start separating His children to mark them as His own, for the window of opportunity for grace is about to be permanently closed. This day, I feel the presence of the holy angels of light all around me. The words that I must know are clearer than ever, for I am privileged to be well-sheltered under His wings and full of His grace. There has never been a time in our history as a civilization that matters more than knowing who Jesus Christ is and understanding 100 percent that if we die today, if we were to die right this instant without truly knowing Him on a personal level, we would be lost and miss out on this once in a lifetime opportunity!

The Holy Spirit has guided me in writing the first book (*My Struggles, My Bondage, and My Freedom and Deliverance*) in order to tell the world what Jesus Christ has done for me personally and how He rescued and delivered me from twenty-six years of struggles and bondage, where the devil took me down the deepest pit. But through all that mess, my God never took His eyes off me because of His unconditional love for me, and now I am being guided to bring a message to humanity in this second book. There are things/events that are about to take place on this earth, and if we are not yet under the wings of God, we will not make it, but those who have already been marked by God to survive these events will be spared.

This day, I suddenly came out of a dream, a revelation like what I thought was in a nuclear war that had been started, as if I could see three hundred sixty degrees all around me. I realized that I was actually in the heavens above, looking down in a vision of future events. What I thought was going up toward heaven was the reverse; the number of objects was as bright white as stars racing through the sky. They were too numerous for me to count, and they were tracking toward the earth. Everyone was in panic mode—running, screaming, and trying to find shelter—yet there was peace within me, for I know that no matter what goes on around us, God is still in control, as He has always been and always will be. I immediately got up from this intense dream. My heart was pounding in my chest. I was confused and disoriented, with one focus in mind and one mission, for I knew that I needed to record these words as warnings from God to bring all who are now sitting on the fence to make the most important decision they will ever make in their lives.

Once again, I say to you that it is not by coincidence that you just heard about this book or just happen to have picked it up. In Jesus Christ, there are no coincidences, but God's reasons and plans for all that have and will become a reality. I will make no apology about this message that must be delivered to our world, as it has been given to me. As I follow the instructions from above to tell the world my life story in my first book, (my struggles, my bondage, and my freedom and deliverance), so shall I continue to listen and deliver this most important message to humanity. There are things so complex within ourselves that the devil does not want us to ever learn and master! We are the most valuable creation of the divine God, so complex that we completely scare Lucifer because he knows we have the master plan deep within our being, and he cannot touch us unless we allow him to do so through our own free will.

Once trapped under his maze of tricks, it could take as long as a lifetime, as we know, to get out of that maze. If we don't get out, it will cost us an eternity in love with our Creator, of whom Lucifer is extremely envious. Yes, Jesus Christ already won the battle for us on the cross at Calvary, but we are allowing the devil to play tricks on us on a daily basis, thus giving him too much power over us. If one is not careful, it may take only an act of God Himself through an angelic intervention and the guidance of the Holy Spirit to bring us back to reality. I have been to at least one of Lucifer's dens, and I will tell all of you that there is nothing nice at all about it. It is so deceptive that our Creator, God, does not love us as much as His perfect creation. Had He not planted certain fail-safe deep within us during creation to retrieve us, Lucifer would easily win this battle over most of the world right now to be worshiped by us as he always wanted. Yes, Jesus

Christ already won the battle for us when He was crucified on that rugged cross at Calvary over two thousand years ago, and He redeemed us as He paid the price for us once and for all. But now the devil will stop at nothing to come after you and me to take us down. As a chosen messenger, I have been commissioned to pass on a message of utmost importance to humanity at a critical time in our history! I cannot and will not ever question what I have been asked to do, for I know deep within my being that I am fulfilling my own destiny as part of humanity.

Lucifer, looking down the stream of time, knew that I was the one to deliver this message to humanity. He set forth a chain of events throughout time and history to stop this message, God's message, from being delivered and awaken all who have been under his spell and control. I cannot express enough the urgency of accepting this message as the truth. Regardless of how much hesitation and doubt you feel, you must fight as you have never fought before and understand that it is something that is legally and rightfully yours, which the adversary is trying to take from you through trickery and deception—something he has had millennia to master. He will become more vicious from this moment forward, for he knows that the time has come for God to start separating and marking His people forever to be with Him. The dreams/revelations have started once again and have gotten intense every night. I am being warned in many different ways, and I feel as if something is trying to stop this message from being delivered. The world teaches us to put ourselves before others, but I say to you that under the wings of God, you are very secure. You are well taken care of and are very safe. You must always look out for others as if you were taking care of yourself, for we are all members of the same family of God.

The events to come in the near future will completely change our way of life. The selfishness of those refusing to accept these words and believe them will become their own downfall.

Now my daily walk on this final journey of the last days on earth represents the final warning of a message that is so very important to be received and understood, with a delicate balance of understanding that can only be achieved through an original, completed promise from the ultimate sacrifice, which has been extended toward our own future and the eternal goal of our Savior, Jesus Christ.

We must believe and live by faith alone; if not, consider this life completely wasted without having learned anything at all and be lost from His presence; being away from God is like being spiritually dead, which might as well be a physical death.

Our selfish nature plays the biggest role in not diffusing this eminent danger of giving up and losing to the adversary on these final days, which will never be repeated by God.

I must not and will not fail to deliver this most important and urgent message from the Most High to humanity! It will 100 percent be carried out. All who have eyes will see. All who have ears will hear! In fact, the last days are here upon us, and the Holy Spirit will touch many lives and allow His presence to be manifested as the final call to bring God's children to a whole different level of understanding in preparation for these unimaginable future events, which have already started and will intensify beyond our ability to understand unless guided by the Holy Spirit.

It is an absolute privilege to have been chosen by the Most High; being a messenger and a servant of the Creator of the universe means everything and is worthy of dedicating the rest of my life here on earth as an obedient servant of God. I am being shown events so devastating that are about to start taking place all over our planet and beyond our capability of stopping, and humanity will come to its knees! The window of opportunity for grace has started its closing rotation on a self-locking hinge, which cannot be reopened as ordered.

The peace within me is so great. My contentment and acceptance of all that is, most could not understand. Following the footsteps of Jesus Christ, the one and only Christ, is second nature to me as best I can, and I am under attack by the adversary to a level I have never seen before. It is, by far, not very easy for me at all. My prayer this day is that through a divine intervention, all who are now ready to be touched by the Holy Spirit, the time is now! Nevertheless, only Your will is to be done, Father, and let this message be understood here and now. In faith, I pray with the power given to me in Jesus's name, and it is done, amen!

There are so many things that I have gotten to understand with the help of the Holy Spirit—things that have been shown to me, at times while I am awake and at other times in revelations like dreams. I am able to understand what to do and how to express it all in a manner that is clearest, so there is no confusion as to what the message is saying.

Two twenty in the morning of August 14, 2010, as it was with the first book, these hours must be extremely sensitive where the link in communications is wide open between heaven and earth or those who have been chosen to accept the task at hand.

The time is so close that I can feel it! There is a march taking place in heaven, and my calmness as I feel it through my body and mind is different; it is nothing I have experienced before.

We must dedicate more time to prayer, not when it is convenient for us but all the time, every single day. I know somehow, some way, the devil will interfere with all plans to pray, etc. But the fight must go on by giving it your all as you invoke the name of Jesus Christ and ask for help from the divine God through Christ Himself, who has given us permission to do so with confidence!

We must always stay close to God and not leave any slack in our prayer cord, which keeps us connected to the almighty God. We must intensify our relationship with the divine by allowing the Holy Spirit to guide and enlighten us, so we may know the truth more than ever.

I have submitted these four letters as evidence to all of humanity, and I stand firm on the fact that we can do much more as a church and not be afraid of what other people will think and say.

I have sent four letters and copies of a book about my own life (*My Struggles, My Bondage, and My Freedom and Deliverance*), a true story about twenty-six years of cocaine addiction and how the devil took me so low, to a point where I had a gun in my hand to kill myself. The Holy Spirit, whom God had sent, intervened and stopped me from pulling the trigger. A true miracle took place that day as God was creating a new chapter in our evolution through my testimony for all whose time has come to be rescued from the adversary in our world today.

To those four men of God who chose not to step out in faith and allow my testimony to be done through them at this particular time, there is no judgment from me because I understand and know that God is always in charge and in control, regardless of all interferences from the adversary! I believe it is for reasons beyond our ability to understand as human beings, and I am positive that it will all work out as per God's plan for all this.

Whether it is their own agenda, selfish reasons, or even fear of what others may think or say, it is still their obligation as leaders in Christ to acknowledge and respond to those stories that will impact other lives if left totally to God alone. That is why prayers are so important in order to defuse all interference from the adversary in a godly time frame.

Our actions dictate whether or not a nonbeliever, a new believer, or even someone who has been around the Word for a while gets to truly know Jesus Christ, stay on track, and grow in Christ!

All the glory be to my Redeemer, Jesus Christ, for having sent the comforter to live within me for enlightenment and guidance, or even I would have regressed and lost faith in the church. Fortunately, in my case, I understand that we all have our own journeys, and, in the end, the will of God will be done as planned.

First Letter Sent Out

04/28/2010

Dear Mr. _____,

I feel as if I already know you because I have listened to you on the air for a while now. I am now a devoted Christian who will follow in the footsteps of Jesus Christ until the day I leave this earth. My heart desires to absorb everything that I can about the gospel, the only true gospel from Jesus Christ, and I want to learn, know, and apply everything in my being to be the closest I can be to my Lord and Savior, Jesus Christ!

I love my God so much, and I can feel the presence of the Holy Spirit within, stronger every day. As I try to walk the path to righteousness, I still feel that I want more and more. I am sharing this with you because this world, as I see it, seems so lost, and the gray areas seem to be as if normal for most, and I want to learn how to show those who are lost how to become a little more open to the truth and get them closer to my God to know who Jesus Christ is, what He was all about, and still is about.

Doctor, my name is Eddy Colin. Two and a half years ago, because of all the trials and struggles I had been going through, the devil took me to a depth beyond anything that I had encountered before and wanted to make me believe that the only way out was to take my own life. But the Holy Spirit, whom God sent, intervened and stopped me just before I pulled the trigger. I also had twenty-six years of cocaine addiction that my God delivered me from in that instant, without help from any doctors or clinics for addiction. I had not been to church for a very long time, and I went that immediate Sunday and spent time with some very good folks that day. The pastor and assistant pastor personally prayed for me in his office, and I know for a fact that God heard that prayer, for I can feel Him every single day in my corner as the Holy Spirit guides me in my new journey.

Out of something so bad, God is now creating a new chapter in our evolution through me with the emergence of my new book, *My Struggles,*

My Bondage, and My Freedom and Deliverance, now being sold all over the world.

My story will bring many who have been lost to Christ. Please accept a copy of my book, and my wish is that you share it with the rest of the world.

Sincerely yours,
Eddy Colin

P.S. There is a one-minute video trailer on YouTube about the book that you must see before you read the book itself. My phone number is _____. Please feel free to call me if you choose to do so. Thank you so much for all that you do! And keep the Word alive on the air, Doctor!

Second Letter Sent Out

Bishop,

I wanted to take the time to let you know how God used your church one afternoon, two and a half years ago. I had my gun in my hand, ready to pull the trigger, and through a divine intervention, the Holy Spirit intervened. I knew I had to call your church, for which I had no phone number. I felt that I had to first dial 1411 in order to get the number for the church before I could call. Through the guidance of the Holy Spirit, I got the number for your church and immediately asked the receptionist to get me a pastor right away because the devil did not want that to happen, but my God is stronger! I was guided through my counselor, the Holy Spirit, to ask for the pastor on duty right away to pray for me because I was about to take my own life. The pastor immediately started praying for the divine light of

God to surround me and protect me from harm. I immediately felt free, as if a million pounds had been lifted off me. Bishop, two and a half years later, I have a published book being sold all over the world, telling my story—my whole life story—and sharing God with millions who may be where I was two and a half years ago when the adversary almost got me. Had your church not been planted in our community by the grace of the Almighty...

I am sending you a copy of my book, *My Struggles, My Bondage, and My Freedom and Deliverance.* Please read the whole book, and when done, I would very much like to come and do my testimony at your church on behalf of my God.

Sincerely yours,
Eddy Colin

P.S. There is a one-minute video trailer on YouTube about the book that you should look at. Thank you so much, and God bless you!

Third Letter Sent Out

Pastor,

My name is Eddy Colin, and I have been listening to your program (a name that I choose to keep anonymous for privacy at this time) for many years. Two and a half years ago, because of all the trials and struggles I had been going through, the devil took me to a depth beyond anything I had encountered before and wanted to make me believe that the only way out was to take my own life. But the Holy Spirit, whom God sent, intervened and stopped me just before I pulled the trigger. I also had twenty-six years of cocaine addiction that my God delivered me from in that instant, without help from any doctors or clinics for addiction.

The thing that keeps a smile on my face is that through all that, my God had a plan that even the devil himself could not comprehend. Out of something so bad, a new chapter was created by my testimony in my book, *My Struggles, My Bondage, and My Freedom and Deliverance*, through which I am sharing my testimony with all whom God has been getting ready for such a message, and they too can write their own story.

I am sending you a copy of my book to read, and I hope someday we can share my testimony on air with others who need to know that our God is still in charge and on his throne. No matter how bad things may get, they must keep their faith and stay in their prayers!

Sincerely yours,
Eddy Colin

P.S. There is a one-minute video trailer on YouTube about the book that you must see before you read the book itself. My phone number is _____. I hope to meet you someday, for you have played a major part in my being here and alive today because of the seeds that you have planted. Thank you so very much for all that you do, and may God bless you always.

Conclusion without the Fourth Letter on Paper for You to Read

Each and every one of those four letters had to be and played a major role in my understanding that we are far from being perfect. We must push harder, as a church, unselfishly and at all costs, to understand that God has called us to bring light to a world of darkness and allow all our testimonies to penetrate such immense darkness and reach all those who may stay lost. Unless the leaders of God's churches truly step out of the box and open their minds to understand that no matter how small or how large a testimony is, the adversary will try to influence your thinking, for genuine testimonies affect him on a larger scale than we can really understand as human beings. It is exactly why we must continuously pray and allow the Holy Spirit to guide us.

Nevertheless, this fourth letter was written very similarly to the first three. The first time, immediately after I almost took my life, that I went to church and shared everything with the pastor on that Sunday, the pastor himself and the assistant pastor prayed for me after the service, offered counseling, and we exchanged phone numbers. But I felt that I was being judged and that they wanted to keep my disaster of a story to themselves and away from the rest of the church. I got one call once, and that was pretty much it. I did not get a response from the letter in question.

As I wrote the first book, there were many tears shed night after night, day after day, in agony and much pain. And now, with my newfound freedom through my Jesus, this level of joy will not be understood by most, and the smiles will never stop, for I know how the story will end. We are on a final stretch of a road that is most complex and can be very confusing, but we must become children once more in our pureness and allow the fragile balance;

thus being guided by our Holy Spirit, who is most essential in order to achieve this critical final journey satisfactorily.

In a dream or revelation this night, or, I shall say, this morning, since it was 5:31 in the morning of August 31, 2010, I saw the elements changing very drastically. The water level was rising, including in the ocean. There was a lot of mud, and it was very windy, but I was not affected, as if I were looking at an event taking place or going to take place. I believe I was looking down the stream of time at a future event that would take place, and even though there was nobody else around as all this was being revealed to me, I heard someone say that it all started in South America and that it was very, very bad there. Suddenly, I was elsewhere among people, and we all knew that the end was very near. I understood how fragile the balance had become and that we must allow the mind and body to stay as a clean temple, or we jeopardize being lost and left out. All of a sudden, people were being separated, like a triage had started. Equipment that was once needed was no longer necessary and was being left behind. I saw an oxygen tank with a clear hose attached being removed because it was no longer needed. The triage continued, as I was to go to another room that

had many, many envelopes with names on them—
names of all who were to continue on. Praise God
Almighty! I found an envelope, and my name was
written on it.

I got up from my bed peacefully out of this
dream, and I understood, without any doubt what-
soever, that this future event that would surely take
place needed to be recorded for all who were awaiting this very message from the divine God.

This day, November 20, 2010, it was 4:15 in the
morning. I had no doubt, nor would I ever question this confirmation from the divine God that I
was on the right path. Even as I observed this most
tempestuous event, where the seawall and levels had
gone up so drastically and were continually rising at
a speed like never seen before by any level of human
understanding as we know things, this dream and
revelation were of an event that would happen in
this lifetime of ours, and no date had been given to
me, for we shall live by faith alone and must repent
of all our sinfulness and our wickedness and surrender to Jesus Christ by acknowledging the ultimate
sacrifice He made for us on the cross of Calvary.

I was down below, observing a hill that seemed
more like a mountain wall—a very, very high mountain peak—and the earth was purging itself through

a constant lava flow. Chaotically below, the people were trapped and could not make it through. I was there through all of it, and my faith was being tested, but under the wings of God, one is always calm and impregnable. Immediately after the revelation of this eminent event that would surely take place, I felt the presence of the Holy Spirit—goosebumps and all with the clarity of mind to record this most important event as a message to humanity.

Discovering the Power Within

Three years later, since my deliverance, I am trying to walk completely within the shadow of Christ, and I am allowing myself to be guided by the Holy Spirit. I should say that as I am being guided by the Holy Spirit, it has taken me to a height that will not be even possible or understood by most unless guided by the Holy Spirit, who is wisdom in its purest form—the source of all understanding, which surpasses all, as we have been taught to believe and understand as human beings.

It is a privilege to have been chosen to deliver this message to humanity, and I pray this day for enlightenment and understanding for all as the window of opportunity for grace is closing.

Understanding the teaching of Christ is a gift, and through the grace of God Himself, one may walk in perfect harmony with the Holy Spirit guiding the way as I have been guided, and every day is a greater challenge to even attempt and try to understand it.

There are so many miracles that God has been performing in my life since my deliverance, and He has blessed me simply because I put all my faith in Him, and it is that simple.

On a daily basis, I talk to God and simply thank Him for life itself, just for taking care of all my daily needs. I never ask for anything because He already said that He will never leave me nor forsake me, and we must just believe and have faith in the fact that He is our Father and that He will always take care of us. One can get rid of stress simply by living a life of faith as such!

I was trying to help someone who was less fortunate than most of us to have a better Christmas, so I took it upon myself to start a small fundraiser to get a few dollars to this someone who had been living on the streets of Denver during the day, and at night, he would settle in this parked vehicle in an alley, in a very dark, unsafe corner, where an automotive body shop is located.

I went to each employee at the dealership, where I now work, and I explained to them the situation. Almost each and every time I started to present the situation to my fellow coworkers, within two to three words out of my mouth to explain the situation, tears would immediately start pouring out of my eyes. I was in deep pain—pain that touched me to the depths of my soul—and I was overwhelmed by sadness, which touched my very essence as a child of God. It hurt so deeply to see someone living in subzero temperatures with nothing, and nobody seemed to care at all, while so many people were having some type of Christmas celebration with senseless gifts—overindulging and wasting money on gifts that their friends didn't even need. Nevertheless, I carried on, for I had to do this! This little girl's mother had brought her to the office that day, heard my plea, went, and found her a little bit of allowance money and donated what she had so that this man could have a better Christmas. My friends, that is pure compassion and love. (God bless you, Olivia. Thank you for your kindness and your pure heart, my child. You will be rewarded in heaven.) Jesus said to let the little children come to Him and do not hinder them, for the kingdom of heaven belongs to such as these (Matthew 19:14).

The one person with the most money in the whole dealership made a mockery of me in his own way and would *not* donate a single dollar even after I tried to explain to him. He said to tell that man to get a job, and he got in his very expensive sport utility vehicle and left the dealership.

That same night, I went looking for that man in the alley. I drove to the spot where I thought he was. It was pitch-black, and nobody was around. It was kind of a scary place to be late at night for anybody, but I needed to do this, for God had pressed upon my heart the need to take care of this.

I parked very close to this shop. There were no lights on, so it was very dark. I called the man's name numerous times but got no answer, so I decided to look around for him while calling his name. He did not answer at all. I had to find him. I would not go home until I found him. I got very close to all those wrecked vehicles that were there and looked through the windows as best I could in the dark-ness, with no results. I walked to this small red car in a dark corner by the front door of the auto body shop, and I noticed that a towel was hung up on the right front door as if to block light intrusion from a light pole across the alley. I decided to knock on the door glass of the car, but there was still no answer. I called his name loudly and said, "It's me, Eddy. Hey, buddy, where are you?"

I walked away from the car for a moment, and as I was walking away from the driver's side of that vehicle, out of the corner of my right eye, I saw a movement of some kind in the back seat of the car. I turned around and went back to the left rear door glass and knocked on it as if I were knocking on the front door of someone's house. Once again, I said, "Hey, pal. It's me, Eddy! Are you in there? Hey, are you in there?" There was finally a motion from within the small confined section of that vehicle, where a back seat once was, but it had been turned into a den, where a child of God then resided at night to attempt to rest and find shelter from the bitter cold of Denver, Colorado's dark and unsafe alley. It was, by far, the saddest thing I had ever encountered in my life. As I write these words with tears in my eyes, I pray to God to give me the strength to carry on and let the story be told so that no child of God should have to endure such a thing.

Finally, the door opened, and it was him—not the way I remembered him at all. He looked weak and old, almost with no strength for a man who was once strong and handsome with all the pride in the world. I had to help him get out of the car, and I could tell that he was in pain—lots of pain from having been all cramped up as he had been. How long had he been enduring such torture? I will never know because he is too proud to reveal his suffering and where his life ended up, and feels as if he is less of a human being. I helped his fragile body to my vehicle that was already warmed up, and we cried and talked for a long while. I gave him the money I had collected for him from my job and a sheet of paper with everybody's signature on it. I told him that God loves him, I love him, and that other people also care. As he tried to read what was written on that sheet of paper, he started crying so hard, and he looked at me in a way I had never seen before. He said to me in Spanish, *"Que Dios te bendiga mi hermano, con todo mi corazon,"* which meant "May God bless you, my brother, with all my heart." I had to make him take the money because he is a very proud man; so proud that it was very hard that even under his present circumstances, it still remains the hardest thing for him to accept help that he sees as a handout, which I explained to him was from God himself through me and the rest of us.

My prayer to God this day is that everyone who touches this book will find within them the light, compassion, and wisdom of the Holy Spirit. Please pray for this man, whom I just spoke about in this book, and for others like him out there, that they will be given the peace that God gives. May they understand the way of Christ before it is too late for them. In faith, pray and believe that this prayer is already on its way and answered, for Christ said that any prayer asked in faith from the deepest part of our being and deemed unselfish shall be answered. I can only imagine the battle, the spiritual battle, taking place right now for our souls on these last days here on earth, knowing how it will all end as I do.

Lucifer had already lost the battle when Christ took it all on the cross for all of humanity. He must be furious, knowing how close his time actually is to facing the consequences of everything he is doing now and all he has done. It is inevitable that the story must and will surely end as it was foretold. Having the guidance of the Holy Spirit as I do and being chosen to merely participate in the writing of these words, I accept! I also understand that it must be my destiny.

As hard as it is for me to write what I am about to say to you all, I must tell you that without a shadow of doubt, I believe this will be my last book, and you must also know and believe all that you have been foretold of our future. I hope you all understand that you still have a chance, under grace, to make it. I pray that the presence of the Holy Spirit is stronger than ever in your lives to help you understand all that you have read.

Believe me when I say that all the things the devil has been offering and giving you will evaporate in the end, and they are not worth losing your soul for. Reach out and ask for help, and help will be given to you. Just have faith in what I am saying to you, for I have lived that life. I have been there, and in the end, it can and will kill you unless you ask God to help you. By coming to the cross, giving yourself up completely, and surrendering all to Jesus Christ, I promise you that it will be the absolute best decision you will ever make. You will be completely transformed into a new person, and people will want to know about the new you. This will give you the opportunity to tell them about Jesus Christ and what He did for you, for us, and for all of humanity.

I am so overwhelmed by *His* majesty, His grandeur, and His infinite love for me, for you, and for all of us, as I am so intensely enveloped. I am allowed to accept and understand how deep this bond with our Creator can be. Oh, how great this God of mine is! How great He is, indeed! Anew He has made me. All that I have become He has made me to be. The rest of my life shall be a living sacrifice for the greatest cause of all, till the end of my days or the day of my Savior's return. The footsteps of Jesus Christ shall be my pathway till the end of my days. Though the storms of life may darken the pathways during my journey, my faith will be my eyes to help me navigate safely as I keep my focus on the cross. Only the cross shall I focus on! For that which you love the most in this world will be your downfall and will cost you eternal life with our King and Savior, Jesus Christ.

One of the well-established auto dealerships and a multimillion-dollar corporation of which I spoke in my first book, and I quote, "There is a march taking place, and God is starting to separate within the auto industry those who are willing to follow the right way and those living in the gray areas of this world." The owners and managers within this corporation have been scattered as they had to close their doors, thus confirming my prediction of such an event. For legal reasons, I cannot mention the name of this company nor give details on this subject, but I trust that my God will grant me the wisdom to deliver his message to humanity as planned.

The Interview

As I continue to write and deliver this very important message to humanity about what I believe to be our last days here, the closest we have ever been to our Savior's return, I embark on my journey to share my own faith with those who may or may not know who Jesus Christ is. My question to each of you is: If you were to die this instant and come face-to-face to give an account of your life with your Maker, and He asked you why He should let you into heaven and gave you a blank notebook to give Him a personal account of your life and tell Him what you have done with what He had entrusted you with and why He should allow you to get into heaven, what would you write down in this notebook of yours?

I was guided somehow to select five individuals. Some of them were friends who had known me since before my release from my bondage of twenty-six years of cocaine usage and a nightlife that involved lots of drugs, nightclubs, and strippers.

Again, my question to each of those friends was: If you were to die this instant and come face-to-face to give an account of your own life with your Maker, and He asked you why He should let you into heaven and gave you a blank notebook to give Him a personal account of your life and tell Him what you have done with what He had entrusted you with and why He should allow you to get into heaven, what would you write down in this notebook of yours?

I told each one of them to take all the time they needed to answer the question, however long it took, and allow the Holy Spirit to guide them, for it would be the most important answer they would ever have to give.

Out of the five individuals, I got one who even took the time to reflect, put something in writing, and gave it back to me! One out of five is not good odds, but it is better than zero.

The answer to God, word for word, that came from one friend of mine:

> In my notebook, I would write one final prayer. It would read something like this:

Heavenly father, I offer no excuses for the life that I have led for I know you were with me every step of the way. The hardest days of my life were the one spent the farthest from you. I am eternally grateful for the days I spent the closest to you, for it is in these days that I came to truly know you. I pray that you will touch my family and friends as you have touch me. Only then can they truly know you. I have shared my life and its story with many. I wish I had shared yours with more. You are the one who truly can understand it for them. In your name I make this final prayer. AMEN.

Wow! Mr. Burton, what a prayer! Thank You, Jesus, for sending us the Holy Spirit, allowing us such a level of faith and understanding, and making such knowledge available to us all! Jesus, I thank You for Calvary once again.

The things that I must endure as personal sacrifices will always remain between the Father and I, and I shall remain strong and faithful for the sake of that which must be—things that most people will never consider sacrificing, but for the sake of this message, a most worthy message that must be delivered, I will suffer that which I must suffer at all costs, and I will not fail for humanity's sake.

I have truly found Christ! Or I should say that Christ found me, and it is a privilege to have the presence of the Holy Spirit within me at all times now. I personally accept that as a fulfilled promise to me and also one that can be fulfilled in your own lives. The greatest thing about such a free gift is that it has already been paid for by Jesus Christ Himself on that rugged Roman cross over two thousand years ago. It is perpetual and will never leave you; as long as you understand, nurture, and respect it, the journey will forever be flawless.

My friends, we have an awesome God to serve—one who wants to give us all we are willing to accept for free—unlike the adversary, who wants our soul as repayment for anything we accept from him. We have completely lost sight of the world, and if I personally have to translate the word *world* or give its true definition as it should be, I will say *one people*. This may sound like news to some, and maybe to most. If we don't even give respect to our own family and our own kind in this world, I must elaborate to clarify our own kind, meaning the human race (all of us of all ethnic groups). If we find it so difficult to get along peacefully without the masquerade, being from the same Father, how then can we learn to respect the validity of the rest of creation, which was thoughtfully placed here for us to live with in perfect harmony? We are using and abusing all our resources to the degree that they have now become irreversible in most cases. We must learn to give thanks and have more compassion for all that our Father in heaven has placed here for us.

At six o'clock on April 24, 2011, Easter Sunday, I celebrate! My Savior has conquered the grave for my sake, for your sake, and for all of humanity's sake. Glory be to our God, forever and ever! Lucifer knows that his days are very near to face the inevitable. He is very restless and has ordered his dark forces on a march, more intense than any other time before. Their missions are to infiltrate wherever they can and manipulate in any way possible to create misunderstanding, rage, dishonesty, drug problems, envy, cheating, fornication, etc. and break families apart one at a time at a very high rate of speed, and they will relentlessly continue the assault on us nonstop.

I know 100 percent that I am on the right path. I know for sure now that I have God's favor because all these negative things that I have just mentioned above, I would love to say, are completely out of my life now, unlike the person I used to be before I found Christ, or, I should say, before Christ found me! But it is still a battle that I must leave at the cross, and I pray daily for help from above to intervene, rescue me, and bring me to safety. Had it not been for the presence of the Holy Spirit guiding me, I would have been destroyed! Had it not been for all the prayers and angelic intervention, I don't know where I would be today. I have been under attack constantly and have been tempted in more ways than I can ever put on paper. I try to shed light, in a way, to try to help you understand, but even I cannot do that! And maybe it is not for me at all to try to figure it out, but the one thing I am sure of is that no matter how many times I stumble and fall, I know that I must and will always get up by the grace of God and only God! And I will continue on this awesome journey, for I know how the story ends.

In the year 2012, there will now be a year of much-needed tests for our world. Our sacrifices will have to be unselfish, and our battles will be tough. But we must know one thing and believe by faith alone that the price has already been paid for on the cross over two thousand years ago by our Lord and Savior, Jesus Christ. For the first time in my life, I am experiencing death up close—the death of my mother. My dearest mother has moved on, and it feels as if someone has just ripped my heart out of my chest and left a big empty hole, a hole that cannot be filled back up with anything. There is at least nothing that this world can fix on my behalf but my faith and the guidance of the Holy Spirit. My faith is strong enough to believe, recognize, and understand in a way that most could not even come close to understanding. It can only happen through the grace of the Almighty God—my God. I would have been a total mess if God had not found me and delivered me out of my struggles and bondage in 2007. There was no way at all that I would be able to survive this great loss I just suffered. At least I would have seen it as a loss, but knowing what I now know through my counselor and guide, the Holy Spirit, it is a grand celebration of victory in Christ. She won against all odds and made it through all the traps the adversary had set before her during her journey here. My mother is victorious because of Jesus Christ's finished work on the cross. Amen, for my God is alive and on his throne!

Thank You, Jesus! I shall be reunited with her again, for the dead in Christ shall live!

The balance of all things is so fragile and beautiful that our God has created many safeguards to ensure that it can never be tempered. One thing with mankind is that they always seek the easy road most of the time, which I believe to be the wrong way the majority of the time. Yes, sometimes God will allow us the easy way, but, ultimately, that easy road is also a test—a test design to evaluate our fidelity to the Almighty God—for when we get on the tough roads, whether we remain faithful or allow the adversary to gain ground once more on us on this most worthy journey. I have been given so much strength at this point in my wonderful journey, and I am so privileged to have such grace from my Creator. I cannot even begin to scratch the surface or even claim slightly, in any stretch of my imagination, or give my own personal views on how magnificent spending eternity with my Creator will be. But I can say proudly that I am grateful to be the recipient of the privilege of being a chosen child of God. Oh, how great is such love—the unconditional love of my Father for me—a love so strong that no mere man can ever understand.

Father, thank You for loving me as You have always loved me. Thank You for never giving up on me when I gave up on You so many times. Through all my disobedience, You would not let go, for such is Your unconditional love for me, for us, and for all of humanity. Without Your unconditional love for me, this message to humanity would never be possible! Yet You knew all this since the beginning of creation, since the beginning of time! Not as we know time, but as You do. Wow!

Guided by the Holy Spirit, under the guidance of the Almighty God, this message is being delivered as per schedule! There are yet many who will need to have this book in their hands, and the Holy Spirit will grant them wisdom to understand this message as good news. I am being guided every step of the way in writing these words to completion through my faith and my faith alone.

Those in our world today will indeed be blind, surely lack godliness, and be under the influence of the adversary, the devil, if they are unable to see that clearly this message is from God and must not be taken lightly. Many generations throughout time have recovered from the vital truth of God taken so lightly, but this message to humanity will be the last and must not under any circumstances be taken for granted as our Creator reaches out to us one more time, not because we so deserve to be saved but because of God's grace and His grace alone.

Ignorance may fail to see this book, *A Message to Humanity*, as being God's final attempt to bring us home safely, while the devil is on his last march, capturing more souls. But if you read carefully and let the Holy Spirit guide you into understanding, victory awaits you since you have been redeemed by the blood of Jesus Christ at Calvary. Leave everything at the cross, and the power of the Holy Spirit all stirred up in these final days will penetrate the hardest and toughest hearts and touch the many who have been awaiting, as the Holy Spirit helps them understand and feel deeper than they have ever felt before, and they will recognize and know the truth.

The same stands true for you today as it does for me! Had my Creator God not been a patient God and ended it all before I got delivered as I did, not only would I have already perished and lost, but I would never have gotten to know who Jesus Christ is and have my salvation today. You would not also have the opportunity to be presented to you now through the reading of this manuscript and be enlightened, as you are at present, thus being redeemed only through the blood of Christ and a sacrifice made for you and me on that rugged Roman cross over two thousand years ago.

In my first book, *My Struggles, My Bondage, and My Freedom and Deliverance*, I said, "On this new journey, many will not be able to follow me!" I now understand more and more that I have been chosen for this, and it is truly my own journey, mine alone, and I accept! Glory be to God in all things.

The paths and obstacles that I must travel are more extreme and more difficult than I could have ever imagined. Yet the peace and control within my inner self are to the highest degree, thus allowing me to stay very stable and in control of all that the adversary is throwing at me in an attempt to try to stop this message from being delivered. These are the last days, as the window of opportunity for grace has already started its closing rotation as per God's order.

In a jail cell, once again beyond my own under-standing, God allowed me to be taken into custody for the sole purpose of rescuing a lost man by the name of Marlow Banks, who gave me permission to use his name and tell the world how he believes that it was no coincidence that I ended up in a cell with him. (By the way, he refers to me as his *cell-e*.) Marlow had been in bondage himself as a drug dealer for years and knew no other way to survive. Yet when I prayed for him, as the presence of the Holy Spirit got stronger and stronger in there, this tough ex-boxer wept. I felt as if electric shots were pulsating through my body, as I had never felt before. I began to weep as my body trembled. Oh, what a privilege it was to know that the God above all gods had chosen me as one of His own! My friend Marlow had been in bondage for many years with the adversary, as you may be right now. But God has a rescue plan in place for you, as He did for Marlow. This man had been lost and under the complete control of the adversary. My God reached in on that day and rescued Marlow, just as He rescued me when I was lost. Amazingly, God also had my release prearranged and preauthorized, with no conviction on all charges, just as He did for me before.

Do not ever question why or how God will use you for the furtherance of His kingdom and His glory because He is God, and He is in control of all that is and ever will be.

I have found myself in a relationship so deep with my Creator that my level of understanding has surpassed all together that of the man I used to be.

As you read this now, the final preparation is being made in heaven. The end is so near that I can feel it.

As I weep for the lost ones—those who will be left behind—I can barely see my own writing through these tears. But I must continue to put all this down, as it has been given to me to write and deliver this message to humanity efficiently and unspoiled, as I am guided to do so. My God, this is so real that I can't stop crying because I love all of you so much that it hurts so deeply to know that so many will be lost and left behind. My feelings are so intense that through all this crying, my jaws hurt, and my face feels as if it is erupting with the muscle contractions in my eyes, and it hurts so much.

If you are reading this right now, God is talking to you specifically and wants you to know that He still loves you regardless of how dirty you may feel. Because of Jesus Christ, you are clean! You are cleaner than you can imagine because, through Christ Jesus, everything is made new because He is life.

I have watched carefully as many people around me stumble, and some have fallen victim to the hands of our adversary as these last days grow shorter toward the return of my Savior. I have personally been tested in just about every way that you can imagine under the sun, and had it not been for the ultimate protection from the angels who have been assigned to protect me as a result of constant prayers and all my supplication to my God, I too would probably have fallen from my Creator and returned to the way I once was. This most important walk has been the most challenging and demanding of my entire life here on earth, and I have been given strength beyond all understanding to endure all that I must for this message, which must and will be delivered to humanity at all costs. I can only imagine what my Savior went through during His walk here on earth—the torments He had to endure in our place for us! Oh, God, what a privilege it is to be what You have made me become today!

When I was in the world, living the way of the world, finding a female partner for entertainment to share the high and flashy life with and have sex with was an extremely simple thing considering I had all the cocaine available to me at a fraction of the price of what others had to pay for the same quantity and higher quality. Getting buzzed on a nightly basis at the strip bars and other places where women go to hang out—all these worldly things that I once enjoyed and lived for are no longer part of my decision-making process anymore, thus making me a prisoner, as some would refer to within my own body! I have so much love to give and so many things that I long for that I have found myself so alone, even though I have someone around me, but our wants and needs are different in so many ways. Yet God has placed me in such a situation to serve. She needs me to be there for her and the kids. I must remain steadfast, and I believe that through the guidance of the Holy Spirit, I will prevail and smile upon what was once and no longer is. Such is my life right now as a new creation, but I have faith that my God will allow me to prevail in the end.

One of the most wonderful things that has happened to me with my deliverance is that back then, as I was cheating on my ex-wife, living a life of deception and lies, because I was living a life of sin, when I found out that my girlfriend (the other woman) was pregnant, I gave her money to get an abortion, but my God intervened for He had a bigger plan for this innocent, fragile little life that I almost destroyed so I could hide my own sinful way. Oh, God, thank You for having been there for me, especially for this beautiful little girl of mine who is now about to turn five years of age. Glory, glory, glory to God Almighty!

The Balance of One's Life

The deepest question any person can ever ask himself or herself, or, should I say, the deepest statement that one would dare make: Oh, how I wish for greater wisdom; it seems so unattainable.

My friends, I am at the crossroads, where I wish I had been more attentive to all the lessons from which I paid no attention to or gave respect. When Christ suffered all that He did for us all the way to the cross, then and even now, so many still do not understand. What was His wisdom then? What is our comprehension now of the wisdom He possessed?

As I seek greater wisdom in my new journey, I unselfishly allow myself to be left wide open for painful events in my life, where I can be hurt deeply, yet I cannot remove myself just to give up on things that are beyond what the eyes and heart can comprehend.

In conclusion, wisdom (greater divine wisdom) is beyond all human understanding and is God's alone because the more you learn, the further away wisdom gets! As you learn and understand more, your mind expands further, thus deepening your level of understanding.

This life here on earth is not long enough for anyone to acquire such a wisdom, which is why we must do everything possible through the grace of God, and through Christ alone can a place be reserved for us in the next round with Christ as our King! Then and only then will we learn and know what divine wisdom is.

Where does a grain of sand come from, how did it become what it is, and why?

Where did that journey start, and can any person on this earth give all the details of such a journey and where it will end up? The answer is absolutely no! Oh, so many mysteries, yet God knows every minor detail of all that was, all that is, and all that will ever be. There are things that neither you nor I will ever know and should be left for God alone to understand. As long as we try our best, and I mean the absolute best that we can, to be a good human being by practicing all that is good and positive and allowing our faith in Almighty God to be our eyes, we will have grace from God Himself, and the presence of the Holy Spirit will be strong within as a guide on this journey, and we will continue to get stronger and stronger every day of our lives.

Had I not been through the furnace of affliction, today would not be possible where I can be sitting here, writing these words of truth to you, so you may as well understand that only through the purification of fire can gold be what it is, and you can cash these words given to you today and now at the Calvary bank of trust and ask for Christ Himself when you get there.

Dancing with the Devil!

There are too many unanswered questions, so many that I want answers to: if part of humanity will be saved and the rest will be lost, and since we are supposed to be close to the end of time as we know time and the return of the Savior, I must know at all costs to myself when and how this God of ours will intervene? Maybe such is the price that must be paid for this message that I truly believe is to be delivered to all who are at the crossroads in their lives and are awaiting such a message in order to understand what they themselves must do as a last effort to gain salvation and be rescued as I got rescued.

I am conflicted in my walk with God since He has been silent for me for longer than I believe I could go on. I have prayed many prayers that seem to have gone into the abyss as my faith shook as it has never shaken before. I have taken a leap into the den, where the devil resides, at all costs to find the answers. I find myself in a dance with the devil, not because I know it is right or that I like it or want it, but because the silence from God has hurt so deeply. My prayers seem to have gone into this abyss, as if God were on the sidelines, watching, waiting, and seeing how far I would go. Yet divine intervention will be fine with me. Maybe what is taking place in my life right now is accomplishing just what it is to be in order to reach out to those who are at their own crossroads in their lives, awaiting for this message to arrive in order to deliver themselves from their own afflictions, and God will have been victorious once again, for it must be so!

I can feel a flicker of faith and light deep within me, waiting to reignite! My head hurts, my brain feels scrambled, and I am so frustrated, wanting to find more answers to this all-time mystery that no one seems to have an answer for, as we seem to live in delusion of a promise that I personally hung on to myself with this hope of a new life far better than what we have now in this world in which we are living. This will either be the biggest hoax that has ever been played on humanity or one of the greatest victories that has ever been known to men since creation or the introduction of mankind into the picture. Where do I go from here? I don't even know myself, but I will continue writing this message and see where it all ends, as I hang on to faith and only faith in my Savior, who paid for my sins in full on the cross at Calvary. So this day, I can stand here with much pride, knowing without the shadow of a doubt that my redemption, my future in eternity with my God/my Savior Jesus Christ, is sealed with His shed blood on that cross for me.

No wishing, no guessing, and at this time, no more prayers about any of this until I see the finish line, where Christ Himself should be waiting with His arms wide open for a message delivered. With a smile, He says, "Calvary paved the roads for you all the way, and you did not have to be so hard on yourself, for I made sure of that at Calvary, and, Eddy, no one can do it alone, which is why the Father sent me when He did and allowed me to take it all upon myself as I did on that rugged cross!" I can feel how severe all this must be, for He rescued me about ten years ago and put me on a path where He structured me and kept me safe as He had angels all around me for protection. No matter what was going on around me, I felt protected and never feared anything, and our relationship grew stronger and stronger through time!

When life almost ended for me, He was my rescue and won my victory over the devil, giving me a new life. Ten years later, I was somehow allowed to leave the safety of my Father's wings and enter the devil's den. Even for the brief moment that I danced with the adversary in his own arena, it was too long for me. I was dancing with the devil once again, and I prayed to be removed immediately as the heavens went silent on me, as if my God had turned His back on me! I dropped on my knees, calling for help. Why? Why? Why? Father, would You allow such a thing to happen after rescuing me ten years ago and giving me salvation? You gave me a purpose and a dream to complete a mission on Your behalf in the writing of *A Message to Humanity*, which I can feel has the greatest purpose since Christ paved the way for this message to be delivered to all whose salvation depended on it.

I prayed, as I have never prayed before. I said, "Father, my faith has shaken to its core, and I feel so completely violated and humiliated. I can never be the same again. How can I continue on this path now? How will I deliver this very critical message to humanity?" I wept convulsively, and my heart shattered beyond return! "Oh, God, please save me once again. Please, I pray that You immediately send me angelic intervention, and may Your divine light surround me and give me peace this instant. Give me peace this instant. Give me peace this instant,"

I repeatedly said. As I slowed down to a calmness that I had never experienced before, I understood it perfectly and could tell that I was not alone!

"There is a price to be paid for anything that is important, especially this message, and you were there just for this brief moment, so others may know the truth and that even when they cannot hear Me, it does not mean that I left them and that I am always there for them, as I was when my own Son felt abandoned on that cross at Calvary."

Notes to All of Humanity!

We are a selfish group of human beings. Of course, most people who will have a chance to tackle such a subject, regardless of their position in this world today, will have so much to say about it. They will be submerged in their own delusions and, most likely, will have their firm, unwavering opinions and probably have their best argument for how they are right on the money in their opinion. Unfortunately, regardless of how they feel, think, and believe, they will be on a path leading to their own destruction! We serve a God who is so merciful, loving, and full of patience and grace, simply for our salvation—a salvation that most of humanity denies being even possible and being a reality. Another percentage of our same world objects to such a thing. The next percentage just totally denounces that such a possibility of being saved by grace and grace alone through the ultimate sacrifice of Christ, the Jesus Christ that I know as our/my Lord, Savior, and Redeemer who died on the cross at Calvary over two thousand years ago paid for our sins in full and redeemed us so that we can be free once and for all.

Of course, we are so immature, as if we were still in our infancy, like babies needing a provider to feed us and provide for our every need. Of course, if we can see what he can see, and I am making a reference to God, our Creator, being who He is, understanding what He can understand, and knowing what He knows, we will be on our knees and giving the utmost praise to Him. What is best for us and our salvation? It is impossible for any mere human to even try to put such a question into perspective and try to answer and understand it. However, Christ gave us the road map to such a mystery, a mystery that God Himself knows that we could never solve on our own, which is why Jesus, God in human form and the second person of the trinity, was sent, or, I should say, came to us, and secured our destiny to spend eternity with Him. Oh, what a great God we serve! Thank You, Jesus, for Calvary, and I love You so much, my Lord.

You are no match against the devil and cannot defeat him on your own. Under no circumstances should you ever taunt him or underestimate his power. Believe what I am saying to you at this point in your life and take it as a warning, so you are prepared for his assaults on you, since I personally experienced it firsthand. He is very crafty and has an arsenal at his disposal to make our lives hell on earth if we are not armed with the armor of God for protection.

I must say that this path that I am on is by far the hardest thing that I have ever had to do or try to follow. On our own strength as flesh and blood, it is impossible simply because the flesh is weak and will fail you every single time. Even when in delusion, you will believe that all is well, but you should know that the devil will most likely have blinders on you. That is why you must allow yourself to stay wide open and accept the guidance and leadership of the Spirit within, who was sent to us as a kept promise by Jesus Christ. He promised because He knew that He would have to leave us here on earth since He had to go and prepare a place for us so that when that time came, we could be with Him also. Without the Holy Spirit as my counselor and guide within me, I could not be writing this message to humanity, let alone having the understanding and knowledge to even know what to write. Oh, what a privilege it is to be part of something so big and so amazing!

My friends, you must embrace your own earthly battles, for they are yours alone to fight. I do not mean that you will be fighting such battles by yourselves and without help. It takes many trials, tribulations, and yes, battles to achieve a level of understanding that will allow you to know that He is with you always. The Spirit is within you to guide you through all difficulties in this life, but you must accept that as part of your inheritance promised to you by Jesus Christ Himself. Without faith and belief, none of this can happen, and your free will allows you to decide one way or the other. But know this: this message is not by coincidence or mere luck that you ended up with this manuscript in your hands today. The devil, your adversary, my adversary, will stop at nothing to try influencing you and can be very persuasive in making you believe otherwise. Under no circumstances should you waiver in what you know, and if you pay attention and listen closely to the true spirit within you, the truth will be revealed to you, and you will know the truth.

At times, you will feel all alone on this road least traveled by mankind, but when it is revealed to you at such times, take advantage of it and spend time talking to your Father in prayers and supplications. By the way, there is no room left for the devil while you are engaging in such intimate or personal time talking to your dear dad. Most of your friends could never understand and are not patient enough to listen to you for that long, and besides, their advice is not as worthy as what the spirit within will reveal to you as a result of your conversation or prayer to your Creator and Father. Only what you are allowed to know can you know, for it is God's alone.

It takes many years of being molded and guided by the Holy Spirit to finally understand that we cannot count on ourselves, our friends, or even our families because, in the end, we will be disappointed, and that means there is only one who can satisfy our every need and help us to stay on the right path and not go into self-destruct mode, which is what this world has to offer. Of course, I, of all people, should know since I resided for a while in such an arena.

Is God silent, or are you just not listening? With all the commotions and distractions all around us in this world, especially with the adversary relentlessly at work and making sure he gets as many as he can take with him, we just need to know that he is never going to stop getting us as distracted as possible since his time is so limited, but you can and will hear God's subtle voice as clear as day if you allow the Holy Spirit to guide you through it all. Pursuing greater divine wisdom and being a student of life is an amazing thing, as it eludes you the closer you get to thinking that you got this! But it only helps you to remember 100 percent that God is always in charge! Christ's death was not in vain. My friends, not at all, and we must remember that no matter how bad the storm seems to be all around us, God is and should be our refuge and our shelter! My faith shall continue to be my eyes until the end of my days! In this race, I will win through Christ, my Lord and Savior. I feel so blessed this day, my friends. God has granted me so much to be grateful for! I cannot see Him yet, I believe. AMEN! Thank You, Jesus, for taking the cross for me and for us, and glory be to You, my King.

Always remember, the glass is half full and not half empty; if someone spills it, there is living water through Christ to be found! On this day, May 10, 2022, after much praying, my faith remains steadfast at 100 percent against all odds, where most would start allowing other thoughts to pollute their minds, but I went back on my knees and pleaded with my God for help because I had nowhere else to go. Sure enough, the call came through, and the lady on the other end of the phone said to me word for word, "I don't know how this just happened, and I do not understand, but we are closing on the house tomorrow. What time is good for you?" I broke into tears. I cannot take these words out of my head now: "Your faith has earned you My grace and My mercy through the blood of the lamb."

Folks, God still listens and will talk to you if you are listening, and He answers our prayers. No matter what life throws at you—good, bad, or ugly—you must keep the faith, for the plan is bigger than what our finite minds can ever understand! (I have lived it, and I now understand.) One hundred percent means 100 percent, and this is what I will give each and every day of my life. I have been given a second chance at life itself since I got hit by a truck at work, where my ribs got crushed and I could not breathe. They had to puncture my right rib cage and insert a tube in my chest cavity to get me air again. They rushed me to critical care at the hospital on January 5, 2023, the same day my dear brother Claude was born back in 1947, and I almost died on that same day. God rest his soul! Is it a coincidence that the day he was born, I almost died or not? I was put on a ventilator to keep me alive for five to six days. Now I truly cherish each and every breath of air that I take, and all the glory be to God himself.

I spent one month in one hospital, one month in another hospital, and four months in a facility for physical, speech, occupational therapy, etc. The devil has mastered one more attack, trying to stop God's message from being delivered to humanity! A most important crossroad is now before me, and it is time that I must cherish and accept the gift of understanding, knowing, and accepting a true path for my life and remembering the words that we must never allow to escape our minds as human beings in search of a firm relationship with our Creator: I will never leave you nor forsake you (Deuteronomy 31:8). Such is a promise we can and should always live by. In fact, it took a tragedy such as this to bring me to the reality that the Holy Spirit had been intervening, and my Creator Himself had been speaking to me clearly. I ignored the calls in my own daily routine until this accident took place, but had it not been for God, I would not have made it, and I would be dead today. This story would never have happened. Fortunately, God has a prepared plan for me, for you, and for all who want to accept His Son Jesus Christ as their personal Savior. In John 14:6, Jesus said, "I am the way and the truth and the life. No one comes to the father except through me."

My prayer for all who are reading this book at this time is this: I pray at this moment that the Holy Spirit will guide you all in the understanding of these words completely, and I will see you in heaven. Amen!

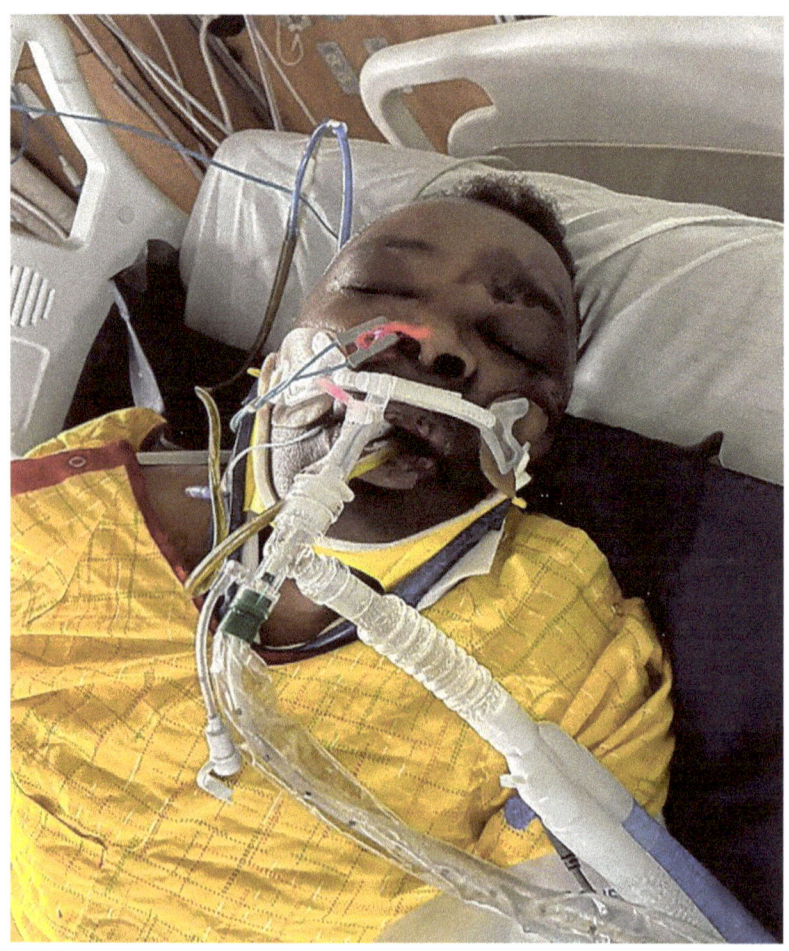

How the devil made a final attempt on my life to prevent this message from getting to HUMANITY

Reading for Christian and Non-Christian!

God's unconditional love for humanity, His grace given to us, and the ultimate sacrifice on the cross at Calvary for our sins in full so we can spend eternity in His presence.

Our world is so dark right now. Even the brightest lights cannot be seen, and that is why this message must be delivered to humanity with angelic protection and divine intervention, for the devil will stop at nothing to try to destroy this message at all costs.

I pray that you are guided by the Holy Spirit to understand all that you must understand as you read this book. It is my most important prayer and request to my Creator in this life. In the name of my Lord and Savior, Jesus Christ, I pray that this message to humanity be understood at all costs. Amen.

The proceeds from the sale of this book will be 100 percent reinvested back to bring lost souls to Christ in these end days, for tomorrow may never come for some of us. I know this to be true because you are reading this message to humanity only by the grace of God, or I would not have made it to this point.

Christians, hold on and never let go of your *faith*! Non-Christians, *God is real*, and *this book will change your lives forever.*

To my friends and family, do not miss out on your last chance for eternity with Christ with no more heartaches and no more pain and suffering.

My Purpose in This Life while I Am Here on Earth

1. Do not focus on only myself ever.
2. Only my Creator God knows the purpose for my life, so I will continue to pray for guidance in everything I do.
3. Being successful by the standards of this world and accomplishing the true purpose of my God's intended purpose for my life are just the opposite.
4. Finding the purpose of our lives individually is to not miss the crossroads when prompted by the Holy Spirit that God is the key, and with Christ, all is possible.

5. The driving force in my life is to get to know God better, understand the moments when I am being guided by the Holy Spirit, and accept the guidance.

6. I know that I have found the true meaning of knowing our God and what He does for our lives, and now that I have found my true purpose, that shall be my mission till the end of days.

7. A message to humanity to bring God's lost children home before it is too late is my God-given purpose.

8. Father God, thank You for where You have placed me to be at this point in my life.

9. The rest of my life shall be a living sacrifice, for it is the right way to be. God rescued me from the world the devil tried to seduce me into! In my life before I was rescued through Jesus Christ, I lived far from God and did not even think about Him. Even then, He kept being my loving Father. Today, living close to God and having found the purpose for my life that He created me for is a privilege, and to deliver this message to humanity, I shall do so for the rest of my life.

10. My Lord shall awaken me from my sleep when He returns, and I shall spend eternity in His presence! I pray for complete guidance from the Holy Spirit within for the rest of my life here on earth to deliver this message for humanity's sake.

God has allowed Donald Trump to become president again in the 2024 presidential election averting something that would have happened in our future, a thing that would have been extremely negative and destructive in this country had he lost the election and not become president, what is to happen in our future now can only and will be prevented by the reach of such a man! It is not for us to understand but God's alone. Trust God always in all things for he truly wants the best for us, our destiny depends on it. There is a reason beyond our understanding why Donald Trump was saved by God from two assassination attempts and today's date is November 8th 2024 1:58, as I am documenting all this which is to be added as part of a message to humanity, I have been prompted by the divine to add this to a message to humanity and I must.

Make today count for there may never be a tomorrow to seize, today is the day to secure an eternal life and I Eddy Colin am now living proof of the grace of God without which I would have forfeited the right to eternal life.

Today of the last days of time as we know time I urge you to seize this moment for it shall not be repeated again, the time is now to show your appreciation for what is good and it shall be yours forever if you seize the time today your chance is now don't let it go by. What must I do to seize this opportunity for I do not know you may ask? but Christ is the way and the road has already been cleared of all obstacles that can hinder you, all is paid for in full by the shed blood on that rugged cross at Calvary over two thousand years ago and the time is now to start on that journey with a once in a lifetime chance that has been given to you while the window of opportunity for grace is still open but not for much longer, we are at the dawn of a new age and the time is now for the marriage supper of the lamb on these last days for we are to be called home very soon.

I was as a seed that fell among the thorns and an angel sent by the grace of God as a bird picked me up and placed me on fertile ground to thrive and be a good servant and a conqueror. When I wrote my first book in 2010 (my struggles, my bondage, and my freedom and deliverance), it concluded like: (Today in my vision, I saw myself laying in an old coffin made out of a tree trunk tied together with straw rope, and I saw myself emerging as a new creation clothed in a white robe carrying a long staff as if I am starting on a new journey. I know without a doubt that the Holy Spirit is within to guide me on this unknown journey. I exhort to you to join me on this new journey–a journey I am taking, still drug and alcohol-free). That vision as I was writing my first book in 2010 was of a premonition of my near death I just now experienced on January 5th, 2023 which is now 13 years later and now I am emerging as a new creation as I saw myself emerging then with this new book: A message to humanity to bring God's children home as they surrender their lives to Jesus Christ before it is too late in these end days as the window of opportunity for grace has started its closing rotation on a self-locking hinge.

As we approach the end of time, God is calling you to make a decision to accept Him as your personal Savior. My prayer for you is to learn to listen to the voice of the Holy Spirit to lead and guide you in the way you should go. Will you answer the call?

www.ingramcontent.com/pod-product-compliance
Lightning Source LLC
Chambersburg PA
CBHW041435300825
31858CB00046B/1992